~A BINGO BOOK~

# The American Revolution Bingo Book

## COMPLETE BINGO GAME IN A BOOK

"The Destruction of Tea at Boston Harbor," lithograph depicting the 1773 Boston Tea Party, by Nathaniel Currier

**Written By Rebecca Stark**

TITLE: The American Revolution Bingo
AUTHOR: Rebecca Stark

ISBN 978-0-87386-470-1

Educational Books 'n' Bingo

Printed in the U.S.A.

# THE AMERICAN REVOLUTION BINGO
## Directions

**INCLUDED:**

List of Terms
Templates for Additional Terms and Clues
2 Clues per Term
30 Unique Bingo Cards
Markers

1. **Either cut apart the book or make copies of ALL the sheets. You might want to make an extra copy of the clue sheets to use for introduction and review. Keep the sheets in an envelope for easy reuse.**

2. Cut apart the call cards with terms and clues.

3. Pass out one bingo card per student. There are enough for a class of 30.

4. Pass out markers. You may cut apart the markers included in this book or use any other small items of your choice.

5. Decide whether or not you will require the entire card to be filled. Requiring the entire card to be filled provides a better review. However, if you have a short time to fill, you may prefer to have them do the just the border or some other format. Tell the class before you begin what is required.

6. There are 50 topics. Read the list before you begin. If there are any topics that have not been covered in class, you may want to read to the students the topic and clues before you begin.

7. There is a blank space in the middle of each card. You can instruct the students to use it as a free space or you can write in answers to cover topics not included. Of course, in this case you would create your own clues. (Templates provided.)

8. Shuffle the cards and place them in a pile. Two or three clues are provided for each topic. If you plan to play the game with the same group more than once, you might want to choose a different clue for each game. If not, you may choose to use more than one clue.

9. Be sure to keep the cards you have used for the present game in a separate pile. When a student calls, "Bingo," he or she will have to verify that the correct answers are on his or her card AND that the markers were placed in response to the proper questions. Pull out the cards that are on the student's card keeping them in the order they were used in the game. Read each clue as it was given and ask the student to identify the correct answer from his or her card.

10. If the student has the correct answers on the card AND has shown that they were marked in response to the *correct questions,* then that student is the winner and the game is over. If the student does not have the correct answers on the card OR he or she marked the answers in response to *the wrong questions,* then the game continues until there is a proper winner.

11. If you want to play again, reshuffle the cards and begin again.

## Have fun!

# TERMS INCLUDED

JOHN ADAMS

SAMUEL ADAMS

ETHAN ALLEN

BENEDICT ARNOLD

ARTICLES OF CONFEDERATION

DANIEL BOONE

BOSTON MASSACRE

BOSTON TEA PARTY

BATTLE OF BUNKER HILL

GEORGE ROGERS CLARK

SIR HENRY CLINTON

BATTLES OF LEXINGTON & CON-
CORD

CONTINENTAL CONGRESS

CONSTITUTION

CHARLES CORNWALLIS

DECLARATION OF INDEPENDENCE

DELAWARE RIVER

FORT TICONDEROGA

BENJAMIN FRANKLIN

THOMAS GAGE

KING GEORGE III

BATTLE OF GERMANTOWN

NATHANAEL GREENE

NATHAN HALE

PATRICK HENRY

HESSIANS

THE INTOLERABLE ACTS

JOHN JAY

THOMAS JEFFERSON

JOHN PAUL JONES

MARQUIS DE LAFAYETTE

BATTLE OF LONG ISLAND

FRANCIS MARION

BATTLE OF MONMOUTH

ROBERT MORRIS

LORD NORTH

THOMAS PAINE

PHILADELPHIA

KAZIMIERZ (CASIMIR) PULASKI

PAUL REVERE

BATTLE OF SARATOGA

SONS OF LIBERTY

THE STAMP ACT OF 1765

THE SUGAR ACT

THE TOWNSHEND ACT

TORIES

TREATY OF PARIS

VALLEY FORGE

GEORGE WASHINGTON

BATTLE OF YORKTOWN

# Additional Terms

Choose as many additional terms as you would like and write them in the squares.
Repeat each as desired.
Cut out the squares and randomly distribute them to the class.
Instruct the students to place their square on the center space of their card.

|  |  |  |  |  |
|---|---|---|---|---|
|  |  |  |  |  |
|  |  |  |  |  |
|  |  |  |  |  |
|  |  |  |  |  |
|  |  |  |  |  |
|  |  |  |  |  |

© **Barbara M. Peller**

# Clues for Additional Terms

Write three clues for each of your additional terms.

_____

1.

2.

3.

_____

1.

2.

3.

_____

1.

2.

3.

_____

1.

2.

3.

_____

1.

2.

3.

_____

1.

2.

3.

| JOHN ADAMS | SAM ADAMS |
|---|---|
| 1. He actively opposed the Stamp Act. Although a great Patriot, this Harvard-educated lawyer defended the British soldiers after the incident known as the British Massacre. 2. This Patriot from Massachusetts played a major role in the negotiation of the peace treaty. 3. He was the first Vice President and second President of the United States. | 1. Because of his strong belief in independence and his ability to persuade others, this founding father from Massachusetts is often called the "Father of the American Revolution." 2. Like his cousin John, he signed the Declaration of Independence. 3. This Patriot from Massachusetts was a statesman, writer, political philosopher, and brewer. |
| **ETHAN ALLEN** | **BENEDICT ARNOLD** |
| 1. He was leader of the Green Mountain Boys, a group soldiers originally founded as a militia to oppose New York's claims to Vermont territory. 2. He and the Green Mountain Boys captured British-held forts at Ticonderoga and Crown Point. 3. Benedict Arnold, who later switched loyalties, fought with him at Fort Ticonderoga in New York. | 1. He and Ethan Allen led the brigade that captured Fort Ticonderoga on Lake Champlain. 2. Although he later betrayed them, he was once to be one of the best generals in the Continental Army. 3. In July 1780, this former Patriot sought and obtained command of West Point in order to surrender it to the British. |
| **ARTICLES OF CONFEDERATION** | **DANIEL BOONE** |
| 1. This document was in effect the first constitution of the United States. It was passed by Congress in 1777 but not ratified until 1781. 2. Until ratification of this document in 1781, the thirteen states were thirteen independent states and not a union. 3. This document was replaced by the Constitution of the United States in 1787. | 1 This pioneer, whose exploits made him a folk hero, served in the Kentucky militia during the war. 2. In 1775 he blazed the Wilderness Road through the Cumberland Gap and into Kentucky. 3. During the American Revolution, he was captured by Shawnees and adopted into the tribe, but he escaped and continued to help defend the Kentucky settlements. |
| **BOSTON MASSACRE** | **BOSTON TEA PARTY** |
| 1. This was the killing of 5 colonists by British soldiers on March 5, 1770. Crispus Attucks, a black man, became the first casualty of the war. 2. This event led to the death of 5 colonists; it was caused by the heavy presence of British troops in Boston because of the Townshend Acts. 3. John Adams defended the British soldiers involved in this incident. | 1. This incident, which took place in Boston Harbor on December 16, 1773, helped to spark the American Revolution. 2. This is the name given to the incident in which men disguised as Indians dumped cargos of tea into Boston Harbor. 3. This event was in reaction to the Tea Act even though the tea was still very cheap. |
| **BATTLE OF BUNKER HILL** | **GEORGE ROGERS CLARK** |
| 1. It would be more accurate to call this early battle of the war the Battle of Breed's Hill. 2. At the ___ Colonel William Prescott instructed, "Do not fire until you see the whites of their eyes." He was trying to conserve ammunition. 3. The ___ took place on June 17, 1775, Although the British, led by General Howe, won the battle, they suffered their greatest losses. The American Revolution Bingo | 1. He was the leader of the Kentucky militia throughout much of the war. 2. He captured Kaskaskia and Vincennes, which greatly weakened British influence in the Northwest Territory. 3. Because the British ceded the Northwest Territory to the U.S. in the Treaty of Paris, he is often called "Conqueror of the Old Northwest." © **Barbara M. Peller** |

## SIR HENRY CLINTON

1. In 1778 he replaced General William Howe as Commander-in Chief for North America. He surrendered his command shortly after Cornwallis, his second in command, surrendered at Yorktown.
2. He was made a lieutenant general and was knighted for his part in the Battle of Long Island.
3. In 1779 he invaded South Carolina and captured Charleston.

## CONTINENTAL CONGRESS

1. The First convened in Philadelphia's Carpenters Hall on September 5, 1774. Twelve of the 13 colonies sent delegates.
2. The Second first met in Philadelphia on May 10, 1775, and adopted the Declaration of Independence on July 4, 1776.
3. In 1781 it became known as the Congress of the Confederation.

## CONSTITUTION

1. It was adopted on September 17, 1787, by a convention in Philadelphia.
2. Our knowledge of its drafting and construction comes mainly from the diaries left by James Madison.
3. This document replaced the Articles of Confederation.

## CHARLES CORNWALLIS

1. His 1781 defeat at Yorktown, Virginia, is generally considered the end of the war.
2. He fought under General Howe in the campaign for New York City; he was then given independent command and captured Fort Lee, NJ.
3. His forces routed those of Major General Horatio Gates near Camden, South Carolina, strengthening the British hold on the Carolinas.

## DECLARATION OF INDEPENDENCE

1. John Hancock was the first to sign it.
2. It said that the Thirteen Colonies in North America were "Free and Independent States" and that "all political connection between them and the State of Great Britain, is and ought to be totally dissolved."
3. It was an act of the Second Continental Congress and was adopted on July 4, 1776.

## DELAWARE RIVER

1. George Washington crossed it in the middle of the night on Christmas 1776.
2. After crossing it, General Washington surprised the Hessian brigade and defeated it at the Battle of Trenton, NJ, on December 26, 1776.
3. After crossing the ___ and defeating the Hessians at Trenton, NJ, General Washington defeated the British brigade at Princeton.

## FORT TICONDEROGA

1. On May 10th, 1775, the Green Mountain Boys, led by Ethan Allen and Benedict Arnold, captured it by surprise attack. Cannon hauled from there helped General Washington drive the British from Boston.
2. In 1777 the American garrison there was forced to leave by General Burgoyne and his men.
3. It is situated at a strategic point in New York between Lake George and Lake Champlain.

## BENJAMIN FRANKLIN

1. He was a printer, satirist, political theorist, scientist, inventor, civic activist, statesman and diplomat. He was Ambassador to France from 1776 to 1785.
2. He wrote and published *Poor Richard's Almanack* and the *Pennsylvania Gazette*.
3. He was Postmaster General under the Continental Congress.

## THOMAS GAGE

1. This British general was Commander-in-Chief of the North American forces from 1763 to 1775.
2. He ordered the British troops to march from Boston to Lexington and Concord in April 1775.
3. He ordered General Howe to attack forces on Breed's Hill outside of Boston on June 17 (Battle of Bunker Hill). The British won, but at great cost. He was sent back to England a few months later.

The American Revolution Bingo

## KING GEORGE III

1. He was the ruling monarch of Great Britain at time of American Revolution.
2. An inherited disease called porphyria caused this monarch to go insane.
3. His insistence on taxing the American colonies to pay for military protection led to hostilities in 1775.

© **Barbara M. Peller**

## BATTLE OF GERMANTOWN

1. Howe and Washington were commanders in this battle of the Philadelphia Campaign of 1777.
2. Washington planned to have 4 units of troops move by night to take the 9,000 British troops stationed here under General Howe by surprise.
3. The Americans lost this Pennsylvania battle when 1 of the 4 troops got lost in the fog and the others failed to coordinate. Washington retreated.

## NATHANAEL GREENE

1. This American general distinguished himself on the battlefields of Trenton, Princeton, Brandywine, Germantown, and Monmouth.
2. He succeeded General Gates as commander of the Southern war theater.
3. Although the British technically defeated the Americans led by him at Guilford Court House, it is called a Pyrrhic victory because of their losses.

## NATHAN HALE

1. Disguised as a Dutch schoolmaster, he gathered information for General Washington on the position of British troops, but he was caught and ordered hanged by General Howe.
2. Before he was hanged he said, "I only regret that I have but one life to lose for my country."
3. He was hanged in New York for spying against British troops on September 22, 1776.

## PATRICK HENRY

1. This Virginian is most famous for his "Give Me Liberty or Give Me Death!" speech.
2. At a meeting of the Virginia assembly in Richmond, Virginia, on March 23, 1775, this famous Revolutionary orator called on the colonists to arm themselves.
3. This famous orator was the first and the sixth post-colonial governor of Virginia.

## HESSIANS

1. These German auxiliaries fought for Great Britain in the Revolutionary War.
2. These German soldiers were surprised and defeated at Trenton by General George Washington and his troops.
3. The Battle of Long Island, which took place on August 27, 1776, was the first battle in which these foreign soldiers participated.

## THE INTOLERABLE ACTS

1. This series of laws was sponsored by Lord North in response to the Boston Tea Party.
2. The ___ included these acts: Impartial Administration of Justice Act, Massachusetts Bay Regulating Act, Boston Port Act, Quartering Act and Quebec Act.
3. One of the___, the Quartering Act, allowed royal troops to stay in houses or buildings if barracks were not available.

## JOHN JAY

1. He became first Chief Justice of the U.S. in 1789.
2. Along with John Adams and Benjamin Franklin, he signed the Treaty of Paris for the Congress of the Confederation.
3. He was the first Chief Justice of the New York Supreme Court from April 1777 to December 1778 and President of the Continental Congress from December 1778 to September 1779.

## THOMAS JEFFERSON

1. He was the principal author of the *Declaration of Independence*.
2. This Virginian was a horticulturist, statesman, architect, archaeologist, paleontologist, author, inventor and founder of the University of Virginia.
3. He was the first United States Secretary of State, the second Vice President and the third President.

## JOHN PAUL JONES

1. When the British captain of the *Serapis* asked for his surrender, he supposedly responded, "I have not yet begun to fight!"
2. He is called the "Father of the American Navy."
3. He was victorious in the battle between his *Bonhomme Richard* and the *H.M.S. Serapis* in the North Sea. Although his ship sank, the British commander was forced to surrender the *Serapis*.

The American Revolution Bingo

## MARQUIS DE LAFAYETTE

1. In December, 1777, This French soldier went with General Washington and his army to winter quarters at Valley Forge.
2. This Frenchman was wounded at the Battle of Brandywine.
3. This French soldier not only volunteered his services, but also obtained further aid in the form of troops and supplies from France.

© **Barbara M. Peller**

| **BATTLES OF LEXINGTON & CONCORD**<br>1. Fought on April 19, 1775, these were the first military engagements of the American Revolution.<br>2. The British wanted to capture and destroy the military supplies of the Massachusetts militia. Colonists were warned by Dr. Joseph Warren.<br>3. The Minutemen inflicted heavy damage on the British regulars here. Their first shot at the North Bridge is called "the shot heard 'round the world." | **BATTLE OF LONG ISLAND**<br>1. Also called the Battle of Brooklyn, it was the 1st major battle after the Declaration of Independence.<br>2. Following victory at this battle, the British won at the Battles of Harlem Heights and White Plains and also captured Fort Washington and Fort Lee.<br>3. The Great Fire of New York occurred shortly after this and the other battles leading to the British capture of New York City. |
|---|---|
| **FRANCIS MARION**<br>1. The British nicknamed him the "Swamp Fox."<br>2. This member of the South Carolina militia is known as the "Father of Guerrilla Warfare."<br>3. He and his men harassed British troops with surprise attacks in which he captured groups of soldiers, sabotaged communication and supply lines, rescued American prisoners and then disappeared into the swamps. | **BATTLE OF MONMOUTH [COURTHOUSE]**<br>1. It is said that during the ___, a woman known today as Molly Pitcher brought water to the troops and took her husband's place at a cannon when he was wounded.<br>2. Major General Charles Lee was court-martialed because of his actions at this New Jersey battle.<br>3. The last major engagement of the northern theater, this New Jersey battle was a draw. |
| **ROBERT MORRIS**<br>1. He was known as the "Financier of the Revolution." Ironically, his life ended in poverty.<br>2. He personally underwrote the operations of privateers, ships that ran the British blockades to bring supplies and capital into the colonies.<br>3. In late 1776 he loaned $10,000 of his own money to pay the troops, enabling Washington to win at the Battle of Trenton. | **LORD NORTH**<br>1. He was Prime Minister of Great Britain from 1770 to 1782.<br>2. In Britain he is sometimes called the "Man Who Lost America."<br>3. The efforts of King George and this man, his prime minister, to save the struggling East India Tea Company led to the Boston Tea Party. |
| **THOMAS PAINE**<br>1. He is best known for his pamphlet *Common Sense*, which advocated independence from Great Britain.<br>2. The fist in his series of pamphlets called *The American Crisis* began, "These are the times that try men's souls."<br>3. He donated his royalties from *Common Sense* to the Continental Army. | **PHILADELPHIA**<br>1. The First Continental Congress convened in this city's Carpenters Hall on September 5, 1774.<br>2. On July 8, 1776, the Liberty Bell was rung in this city so citizens could hear the first public reading of the Declaration of Independence.<br>3. The Battle of Brandywine was fought on September 11, 1777, to stop British troops from reaching this temporary American capital. |
| **KAZIMIERZ (CASIMIR ) PULASKI**<br>1. This Polish soldier became a general in the Continental Army.<br>2. This Polish soldier took part in the Battle of Brandywine, the Siege of Charleston, and the Battle of Savannah. He died from wounds he received at the Battle of Savannah.<br>3. This Polish soldier is sometimes called the "Father of the American cavalry."<br>The American Revolution Bingo | **PAUL REVERE**<br>1. He and William Dawes were instructed by Dr. Joseph Warren to ride from Boston to Lexington to warn John Hancock and Samuel Adams of the movements of the British Army.<br>2. This silversmith from Boston was active in the Sons of Liberty.<br>3. Henry Wadsworth Longfellow's poem made his "Midnight Ride" famous.<br>© **Barbara M. Peller** |

| | |
|---|---|
| **BATTLE OF SARATOGA**<br>1. This New York battle is considered the turning point in the war because the American victory here convinced France to enter the war as an ally.<br>2. There were really 2 battles: 1 on September 19 and 1 on October7, 1777. General John Burgoyne and his army retreated and then surrendered.<br>3. There were actually 2 battles here: the Battle of Freeman's Farm and the Battle of Bemis Heights. | **SONS OF LIBERTY**<br>1. This secret organization of American Patriots was sometimes referred to as "Sons of Violence" by the British and the Loyalists.<br>2. They set up Committees of Correspondence to coordinate action against Great Britain.<br>3. One of the most important members of this secret organization was James Otis. He is credited with saying, "Taxation without representation is tyranny." |
| **THE STAMP ACT OF 1765**<br>1. This act required legal documents, permits, contracts, newspapers, wills, pamphlets, and playing cards in the colonies to carry a tax stamp.<br>2. It was Britain's first real attempt to impose a direct tax on the colonies in order to raise money.<br>3. This act was meant to defray the expenses of "defending, protecting, and securing the British colonies and plantations in America." | **THE SUGAR ACT**<br>1. This 1764 act put a tax on foreign refined sugar and increased taxes on coffee, indigo, and certain kinds of wine.<br>2. It was a modified version of the Sugar and Molasses Act of 1733, which was about to expire.<br>3. Although this act cut in half the tax that had been imposed by the Sugar and Molasses Act, this time the government intended to collect it. |
| **THE TOWNSHEND ACT**<br>1. It was named after the British Chancellor of the Exchequer, or Treasurer. It placed new taxes on glass, lead, paints, paper, and tea.<br>2. Britain eventually repealed all the taxes imposed by this 1767 act except the one on tea.<br>3. In reaction to this act Bostonians established non-importation agreements that spread throughout the colonies. British Merchants again interceded. | **TORIES**<br>1. During the American Revolution, this term was used to described Loyalists, colonists who sided with Great Britain against the revolutionaries.<br>2. Rebels sometimes made examples of these Loyalists by tarring and feathering them.<br>3. Walter Butler was one. He was captured by Continental Army troops while trying to recruit rangers in German Flatts, New York, but escaped. |
| **TREATY OF PARIS**<br>1. This document formally ended the United States War for Independence.<br>2. This document was signed by John Adams, Benjamin Franklin and John Jay for the U.S. and by David Hartley, a member Parliament, as a representative of King George III.<br>3. The American Congress of the Confederation ratified this document on January 14, 1784. | **VALLEY FORGE**<br>1. In Pennsylvania, it was the site of the camp of the American Continental Army over the harsh winter of 1777–1778.<br>2. Baron Friedrich von Steuben helped train the troops here during the winter of 1777–1778.<br>3. Washington's troops camped here during the winter of 1777–1778; they were undernourished and poorly clothed and suffered from disease. |
| **GEORGE WASHINGTON**<br>1. He led the Continental Army to victory over Great Britain in the American Revolution.<br>2. He later became the first President of the United States.<br>3. Henry Lee III, a cavalry officer known as "Light Horse Harry," wrote this about him: "First in war, first in peace, and first in the hearts of his countrymen."<br>The American Revolution Bingo | **BATTLE OF YORKTOWN**<br>1. The surrender of Cornwallis's army here prompted the British government to eventually negotiate an end to the conflict.<br>2. This battle in Virginia was the last major battle of the American Revolutionary War.<br>3. On October 19, 1781, British troops under General Cornwallis surrendered to General Washington's combined American & French army.<br>© **Barbara M. Peller** |

# The American Revolution Bingo

| | | | | |
|---|---|---|---|---|
| Delaware River | John Adams | Daniel Boone | Nathan Hale | Thomas Jefferson |
| Boston Massacre | Sam Adams | Tories | Marquis de Lafayette | Valley Forge |
| Ethan Allen | Battle of Yorktown | | Battle of Monmouth | Sir Henry Clinton |
| Sons of Liberty | Declaration of Independence | George Washington | Hessians | Francis Marion |
| Lord North | Thomas Gage | Paul Revere | Treaty of Paris | The Sugar Act |

# The American Revolution Bingo

| | | | | |
|---|---|---|---|---|
| Sons of Liberty | Ethan Allen | John Paul Jones | The Stamp Act of 1765 | Nathanael Greene |
| Francis Marion | Continental Congress | Benedict Arnold | Boston Tea Party | The Intolerable Acts |
| Battles of Lexington & Concord | Thomas Gage | | Fort Ticonderoga | George Washington |
| Philadelphia | Robert Morris | Battle of Yorktown | Kazimierz (Casimir) Pulaski | The Sugar Act |
| Valley Forge | Tories | Paul Revere | Boston Massacre | Treaty of Paris |

# The American Revolution Bingo

| Sons of Liberty | George Washington | Continental Congress | Hessians | Ethan Allen |
|---|---|---|---|---|
| Marquis de Lafayette | Sam Adams | George Rogers Clark | John Adams | Boston Tea Party |
| Declaration of Independence | Tories |  | The Intolerable Acts | Articles of Confederation |
| Battle of Yorktown | Battles of Lexington & Concord | Lord North | Philadelphia | John Paul Jones |
| Treaty of Paris | Boston Massacre | Paul Revere | Kazimierz (Casimir) Pulaski | Nathanael Greene |

# The American Revolution Bingo

| | | | | |
|---|---|---|---|---|
| Battle of Yorktown | The Intolerable Acts | Daniel Boone | Boston Tea Party | Nathanael Greene |
| John Jay | Battle of Bunker Hill | John Adams | The Stamp Act of 1765 | Ethan Allen |
| Battle of Monmouth | Philadelphia | | Thomas Jefferson | Nathan Hale |
| George Washington | Constitution | Tories | Paul Revere | Benedict Arnold |
| Boston Massacre | Valley Forge | Robert Morris | Treaty of Paris | Sir Henry Clinton |

# The American Revolution Bingo

| | | | | |
|---|---|---|---|---|
| Valley Forge | Thomas Jefferson | Declaration of Independence | Benedict Arnold | Boston Massacre |
| John Jay | George Washington | George Rogers Clark | Fort Ticonderoga | Sam Adams |
| Daniel Boone | Sir Henry Clinton | | Marquis de Lafayette | King George III |
| The Sugar Act | Nathanael Greene | Delaware River | Kazimierz (Casimir) Pulaski | Charles Cornwallis |
| Continental Congress | Paul Revere | Ethan Allen | Battle of Yorktown | Battle of Monmouth |

# The American Revolution Bingo

| | | | | |
|---|---|---|---|---|
| Articles of Confederation | The Intolerable Acts | John Paul Jones | Nathanael Greene | Sir Henry Clinton |
| Hessians | Declaration of Independence | Charles Cornwallis | John Adams | Ethan Allen |
| The Stamp Act of 1765 | Boston Tea Party | | Battle of Bunker Hill | Fort Ticonderoga |
| Paul Revere | Lord North | Kazimierz (Casimir) Pulaski | Robert Morris | Daniel Boone |
| Francis Marion | Benedict Arnold | Delaware River | Battle of Monmouth | Constitution |

# The American Revolution Bingo

| Delaware River | The Intolerable Acts | King George III | Marquis de Lafayette | Continental Congress |
|---|---|---|---|---|
| Francis Marion | Nathanael Greene | Thomas Gage | Sam Adams | John Jay |
| John Paul Jones | Nathan Hale | | Fort Ticonderoga | Battle of Bunker Hill |
| Battle of Yorktown | Philadelphia | George Rogers Clark | Sons of Liberty | Battles of Lexington & Concord |
| Paul Revere | Boston Massacre | Kazimierz (Casimir) Pulaski | Robert Morris | Articles of Confederation |

# The American Revolution Bingo

| Battle of Monmouth | The Intolerable Acts | Benjamin Franklin | Hessians | Battle of Bunker Hill |
|---|---|---|---|---|
| John Jay | Daniel Boone | The Stamp Act of 1765 | Sir Henry Clinton | Benedict Arnold |
| Constitution | Thomas Paine |  | Nathanael Greene | Thomas Jefferson |
| Treaty of Paris | Battle of Yorktown | Sons of Liberty | Boston Tea Party | Philadelphia |
| Tories | Paul Revere | Robert Morris | Declaration of Independence | Francis Marion |

# The American Revolution Bingo

| Fort Ticonderoga | Continental Congress | Thomas Gage | Constitution | Boston Massacre |
|---|---|---|---|---|
| Boston Tea Party | Nathanael Greene | Battle of Monmouth | Declaration of Independence | The Intolerable Acts |
| Patrick Henry | Delaware River | | Sam Adams | Benjamin Franklin |
| Charles Cornwallis | The Sugar Act | Lord North | Marquis de Lafayette | King George III |
| Philadelphia | Kazimierz (Casimir) Pulaski | George Rogers Clark | Sons of Liberty | Thomas Jefferson |

# The American Revolution Bingo

| Sons of Liberty | Hessians | Battle of Bunker Hill | The Stamp Act of 1765 | Constitution |
|---|---|---|---|---|
| Sir Henry Clinton | Benedict Arnold | John Adams | Sam Adams | Nathanael Greene |
| Thomas Paine | The Intolerable Acts | | Nathan Hale | Battles of Lexington & Concord |
| Lord North | The Sugar Act | Charles Cornwallis | Kazimierz (Casimir) Pulaski | Patrick Henry |
| George Rogers Clark | Francis Marion | John Paul Jones | Valley Forge | Battle of Monmouth |

# The American Revolution Bingo

| | | | | |
|---|---|---|---|---|
| Articles of Confederation | The Intolerable Acts | Declaration of Independence | Charles Cornwallis | Francis Marion |
| Benjamin Franklin | Patrick Henry | Marquis de Lafayette | Fort Ticonderoga | John Adams |
| John Jay | Nathanael Greene | | John Paul Jones | Thomas Gage |
| George Rogers Clark | Hessians | Kazimierz (Casimir) Pulaski | Boston Massacre | Sons of Liberty |
| Boston Tea Party | Paul Revere | Delaware River | Robert Morris | Continental Congress |

# The American Revolution Bingo

| | | | | |
|---|---|---|---|---|
| Continental Congress | Thomas Jefferson | Patrick Henry | Hessians | Fort Ticonderoga |
| Thomas Gage | Francis Marion | Daniel Boone | Robert Morris | Sam Adams |
| Delaware River | King George III | | Sir Henry Clinton | The Stamp Act of 1765 |
| Paul Revere | Philadelphia | Nathanael Greene | Sons of Liberty | John Jay |
| The Intolerable Acts | Benjamin Franklin | Thomas Paine | Boston Tea Party | Benedict Arnold |

# The American Revolution Bingo

| Charles Cornwallis | Thomas Jefferson | Articles of Confederation | Patrick Henry | Sir Henry Clinton |
|---|---|---|---|---|
| Daniel Boone | Benjamin Franklin | Nathanael Greene | Fort Ticonderoga | Battles of Lexington & Concord |
| Hessians | Continental Congress | | Thomas Gage | King George III |
| Battle of Monmouth | Kazimierz (Casimir) Pulaski | Battle of Bunker Hill | Thomas Paine | Sons of Liberty |
| Paul Revere | The Sugar Act | Robert Morris | Delaware River | Marquis de Lafayette |

# The American Revolution Bingo

| Boston Massacre | Nathanael Greene | Declaration of Independence | Fort Ticonderoga | Boston Tea Party |
|---|---|---|---|---|
| Benedict Arnold | Delaware River | Patrick Henry | Sam Adams | The Intolerable Acts |
| Charles Cornwallis | Nathan Hale | | John Paul Jones | George Rogers Clark |
| The Sugar Act | Kazimierz (Casimir) Pulaski | Thomas Paine | Battle of Bunker Hill | Articles of Confederation |
| Paul Revere | The Stamp Act of 1765 | Battles of Lexington & Concord | Francis Marion | Battle of Monmouth |

# The American Revolution Bingo

| Marquis de Lafayette | Fort Ticonderoga | Declaration of Independence | Continental Congress | Hessians |
|---|---|---|---|---|
| Articles of Confederation | John Paul Jones | John Adams | Daniel Boone | Boston Tea Party |
| Sir Henry Clinton | Delaware River | | Ethan Allen | The Intolerable Acts |
| Paul Revere | Patrick Henry | Benjamin Franklin | Kazimierz (Casimir) Pulaski | Charles Cornwallis |
| Francis Marion | Philadelphia | Robert Morris | Constitution | Thomas Gage |

# The American Revolution Bingo

| | | | | |
|---|---|---|---|---|
| Battle of Bunker Hill | Patrick Henry | Benjamin Franklin | Constitution | Battle of Saratoga |
| The Stamp Act of 1765 | Battles of Lexington & Concord | King George III | John Jay | Nathan Hale |
| Charles Cornwallis | Thomas Jefferson | | Sir Henry Clinton | Thomas Gage |
| Battle of Yorktown | Benedict Arnold | Paul Revere | Battle of Long Island | Sons of Liberty |
| Boston Tea Party | The Townshend Act | Robert Morris | Philadelphia | The Intolerable Acts |

# The American Revolution Bingo

| George Rogers Clark | Battle of Long Island | Battle of Germantown | Patrick Henry | Boston Massacre |
|---|---|---|---|---|
| Marquis de Lafayette | Boston Tea Party | Kazimierz (Casimir) Pulaski | Nathan Hale | King George III |
| Fort Ticonderoga | Battle of Monmouth |  | The Townshend Act | Benjamin Franklin |
| The Sugar Act | Francis Marion | Sons of Liberty | Declaration of Independence | Battles of Lexington & Concord |
| Lord North | Charles Cornwallis | Continental Congress | Hessians | Thomas Jefferson |

# The American Revolution Bingo

| Constitution | Thomas Paine | Benedict Arnold | Charles Cornwallis | The Stamp Act of 1765 |
|---|---|---|---|---|
| The Intolerable Acts | George Rogers Clark | Lord North | Sir Henry Clinton | Boston Tea Party |
| Fort Ticonderoga | Battles of Lexington & Concord | | Battle of Germantown | Daniel Boone |
| The Sugar Act | John Adams | Kazimierz (Casimir) Pulaski | Sons of Liberty | John Paul Jones |
| The Townshend Act | Patrick Henry | Declaration of Independence | Battle of Long Island | Articles of Confederation |

# The American Revolution Bingo

| Sir Henry Clinton | Articles of Confederation | Patrick Henry | Benjamin Franklin | Sir Henry Clinton |
|---|---|---|---|---|
| Marquis de Lafayette | Hessians | The Intolerable Acts | Continental Congress | Nathan Hale |
| Battle of Long Island | Boston Massacre | | Sam Adams | Ethan Allen |
| John Paul Jones | The Townshend Act | Lord North | Philadelphia | Battle of Germantown |
| Daniel Boone | Battle of Saratoga | Francis Marion | Battle of Monmouth | Robert Morris |

© Barbara M. Peller

# The American Revolution Bingo

| Thomas Paine | Battle of Long Island | Hessians | Patrick Henry | Robert Morris |
|---|---|---|---|---|
| Benedict Arnold | Thomas Gage | John Jay | Lord North | The Stamp Act of 1765 |
| Thomas Jefferson | King George III | | Battle of Yorktown | John Adams |
| Valley Forge | Tories | Treaty of Paris | Philadelphia | The Townshend Act |
| George Washington | Battle of Monmouth | Battle of Saratoga | Sons of Liberty | Battle of Germantown |

# The American Revolution Bingo

| Constitution | John Paul Jones | Battle of Germantown | Daniel Boone | Charles Cornwallis |
|---|---|---|---|---|
| The Stamp Act of 1765 | Hessians | Ethan Allen | Benjamin Franklin | Sam Adams |
| Benedict Arnold | Nathan Hale | | Delaware River | King George III |
| The Townshend Act | The Sugar Act | Philadelphia | John Adams | Boston Massacre |
| Battle of Saratoga | George Rogers Clark | Battle of Long Island | Battles of Lexington & Concord | John Jay |

# The American Revolution Bingo

| | | | | |
|---|---|---|---|---|
| Battle of Bunker Hill | Battle of Long Island | Continental Congress | Daniel Boone | Robert Morris |
| Articles of Confederation | Thomas Paine | Francis Marion | Marquis de Lafayette | John Adams |
| John Paul Jones | Charles Cornwallis | | Treaty of Paris | Delaware River |
| Battles of Lexington & Concord | Battle of Saratoga | The Townshend Act | George Rogers Clark | Philadelphia |
| Valley Forge | Tories | Battle of Monmouth | Lord North | Battle of Germantown |

# The American Revolution Bingo

| | | | | |
|---|---|---|---|---|
| Battle of Bunker Hill | Thomas Paine | Boston Massacre | Battle of Long Island | Benjamin Franklin |
| Battle of Germantown | Robert Morris | John Jay | The Stamp Act of 1765 | Delaware River |
| King George III | Constitution | | Charles Cornwallis | Battles of Lexington & Concord |
| Valley Forge | Treaty of Paris | The Townshend Act | George Rogers Clark | Thomas Jefferson |
| George Washington | Battle of Yorktown | Battle of Saratoga | Hessians | Tories |

# The American Revolution Bingo

| Battle of Yorktown | John Jay | Battle of Long Island | Declaration of Independence | Battle of Germantown |
|---|---|---|---|---|
| John Adams | The Sugar Act | Marquis de Lafayette | Battle of Bunker Hill | Sam Adams |
| Thomas Jefferson | Benjamin Franklin |  | Treaty of Paris | The Townshend Act |
| Ethan Allen | Valley Forge | Tories | Battle of Saratoga | Nathan Hale |
| Robert Morris | Boston Massacre | Benedict Arnold | Boston Tea Party | George Washington |

# The American Revolution Bingo

| | | | | |
|---|---|---|---|---|
| Battle of Germantown | Battle of Long Island | John Paul Jones | The Stamp Act of 1765 | Constitution |
| Lord North | Hessians | Benjamin Franklin | Thomas Paine | Battle of Bunker Hill |
| The Sugar Act | Treaty of Paris | | Nathan Hale | Battle of Yorktown |
| George Rogers Clark | Daniel Boone | Valley Forge | Battle of Saratoga | The Townshend Act |
| King George III | Boston Tea Party | Declaration of Independence | Tories | George Washington |

# The American Revolution Bingo

| | | | | |
|---|---|---|---|---|
| John Paul Jones | Benedict Arnold | Battle of Long Island | Thomas Paine | Thomas Gage |
| Valley Forge | Treaty of Paris | Marquis de Lafayette | The Townshend Act | Sam Adams |
| Kazimierz (Casimir) Pulaski | Tories | | Battle of Saratoga | Battle of Yorktown |
| Constitution | Articles of Confederation | John Jay | George Washington | John Adams |
| Boston Tea Party | Nathan Hale | Battle of Germantown | Ethan Allen | King George III |

# The American Revolution Bingo

| Sir Henry Clinton | Thomas Paine | Ethan Allen | Battle of Long Island | Battle of Bunker Hill |
|---|---|---|---|---|
| Thomas Gage | Battle of Germantown | Treaty of Paris | The Stamp Act of 1765 | Nathan Hale |
| Tories | Battles of Lexington & Concord |  | King George III | Lord North |
| Sons of Liberty | Constitution | Francis Marion | Battle of Saratoga | The Townshend Act |
| Daniel Boone | Fort Ticonderoga | Boston Tea Party | George Washington | Valley Forge |

# The American Revolution Bingo

| Battle of Germantown | Thomas Paine | Constitution | Marquis de Lafayette | Fort Ticonderoga |
|---|---|---|---|---|
| The Sugar Act | Lord North | John Jay | King George III | Ethan Allen |
| Thomas Jefferson | Treaty of Paris |  | Sam Adams | Battle of Long Island |
| Declaration of Independence | Valley Forge | Nathanael Greene | Battle of Saratoga | The Townshend Act |
| Boston Tea Party | Benjamin Franklin | George Washington | Articles of Confederation | Tories |

© **Barbara M. Peller**

# The American Revolution Bingo

| Boston Massacre | Battle of Long Island | The Stamp Act of 1765 | Fort Ticonderoga | The Townshend Act |
|---|---|---|---|---|
| John Adams | Thomas Paine | John Paul Jones | Nathan Hale | Sam Adams |
| The Sugar Act | Charles Cornwallis | | King George III | John Jay |
| George Washington | Articles of Confederation | Daniel Boone | Battle of Saratoga | Treaty of Paris |
| Valley Forge | Continental Congress | Tories | Battle of Germantown | Ethan Allen |